Unhexing
And
Jinx Removing

By Donna Rose

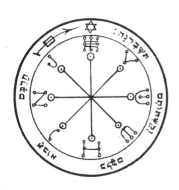

UNHEXING AND JINX REMOVING
By Donna Rose

© ORIGINAL PUBLICATIONS 2004

ISBN: 0-942272-84-6

FIRST EDITION
First Printing 2004

Original Publications
P.O. Box 236
Old Bethpage, New York 11804-0236
(516) 454-6809

Printed in the United States of America

Table of Contents

Prayer for Protection   4

Introduction   5

Rituals for Unhexing and Jinx Removing   7

Herbs, Oils, Incense, Powders, Floorwashes and   23
Salts

    Herbs   23
    Oils   25
    Incense   28
    Powders   28
    Floorwashes and Salts   29

Seals   31

Table of Astral Colors   36

Miscellany of Uncrossing   36

Colors of Jinx Removing   37

Numbers   37

Prayer For Protection

*I dwell in the bright, divine light,
all goodness is attracted to me for my highest good.
I am attuned with divine love and divine goodness.
I give thanks for the divine light.*

Introduction

This is a booklet of easy-to-do unhexing and jinx removing spells. The rituals and information contained in it will help you to secure your peace of mind. You can be assured that you have the power to protect yourself from the negativity you are exposed to on a daily basis, from both known and unknown sources.

You have the ability to control your thoughts and help fulfill your direction and simplicity of life. You need a *"Point of Concentration"* to do this, and to assist you in sending your own thoughts and in the protection of your physical body.

Seals, talismans, stones and candleburning rituals all have magical powers within themselves, but, with your positive thinking, action, and various useful means, this power grows stronger.

The following rituals for jinx removing and uncrossing are strongest when done on a Sunday at 1 o'clock in the afternoon. The sun is the "planet" for this power, and rules over Sunday. Three is the number which is the strongest for this purpose; it rules over uncrossing.

The rituals combined with the charms can be used together; when all the elements are used in combinations, they develop a very strong Power.

Much research has been done to compile this booklet, and the information here gathered and presented will give you that *"Point of Concentration"* which will clear your life and keep it that way.

May the Love of the Supreme Being be yours!
With love from me to you...

Rituals for Unhexing and Jinx Removing

The magical power of candle burning has long been known to those who have sought Power in many faiths. In combination with herbs, oils, powders and incenses, the power available is staggering.

Candles are used on birthday cakes, in churches, and even for personal pleasure. The use of fire has been a matter of history, the oldest indication we have is of cave people using fire to protect their caves. The practice remains today - we may still use the fire of candles for protection.

An analysis of the procedure reveals that the simple Candle Rite is a mixture of two of the basics of all magical rituals: (1) Concentration of the mind; and (2) A symbol on which to focus the attention.

The Spiritual appeal coupled with the aesthetic is one of the basic uses of candles characteristic of almost all people. Light is symbolic of Truth and we consider the flame as Light. Candle burning is a simple magical rite and does not necessarily involve other items to obtain the request. You have to use your own powers of concentration, mind determination, will and desire to obtain what you want.

The procedure is simple; all that is required for success is a candle, determination, a purpose, and a concentrated force of energy toward the objective or desire of the individual.

The candle is, of course, the most important item of the rite.

However, candles come in all shapes, sizes and colors, and you must determine which is the best for you and your purpose.

Homemade candles are the best to use, made of pure beeswax. If that is not possible, then it becomes necessary to purchase the candles. It must be pointed out that a candle can be used only once, for a single purpose, then discarded (if not burned up). The candle cannot be used over and over again for any purpose except the original one

Your state of mind is the most important magical power of all. Positive thinking while burning the candles in a properly set up ritual insures the success of your endeavors, the fulfillment of your wish.

Charging the Candles

This procedure consists of rubbing the candle in a certain manner, while concentrating deeply on your purpose or petition, and strongly visualizing the desired outcome. The medium of transference, via which you will impress those thoughts into the candle, is your Occult Oil, chosen for each individual purpose.

FOR GLASS ENCLOSED CANDLES: Pour a few drops of the oil into the candle jar. With the first two fingers, rub the oil into the wax. If the candle is for **banishing** purposes, rub in a clockwise (deosil) circular direction. If the purpose is to **attract** or draw something closer to you, rub in a counterclockwise (widdershins) circular direction. Concentrate your thoughts on the desired outcome. Continue the operation until you can no longer hold the thought-picture in mind. Finish by sealing the candle with a Solar Cross or Pentagram drawn on the glass with the forefinger dipped in the oil.

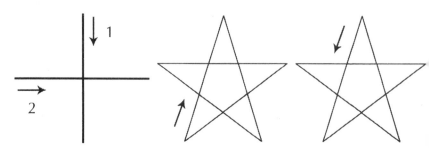

Wipe your hands clean of the oil on a paper or linen towel. If you are doing several candles with different types of oils, clean the hands between operations with a cloth saturated in rubbing alcohol, or one of the sprinkling waters.

FOR PLAIN WAX CANDLES: If the purpose of the candle is to banish something, for instance, to drive away undesirable influences or conditions, or to get rid of an illness, etc... Begin by pouring a few drops of the oil into the palm of your hand. Rub the surface of the candle from the center toward the bottom. Then rub from the center toward the top. Concentrate deeply on your desired outcome. Be sure to hold a clear picture in the mind of the event happening as you wish it.

FOR ASTRAL OR IMAGE CANDLES: Representing yourself, or other persons: The method of anointing these candles will follow the same rules as for straight candles, but the concentration should be along these lines: *"Here stands the image of (me, "George," "Mary," etc.) It thinks as I think, moves as I wish it to move, behaves as I wish it to behave... and by my hand **lives** as the true person."* At this point, hold the candle up to your mouth and breathe upon it, saying: *"Breathe now (name of person) and receive the gift of the Spirit."* In some cases it may be, *"Breathe now, and receive the gift of life - feel the blessing of vibrant health radiating upon you . . . etc."*

Lighting Your Candles

Matches on an altar are taboo. The reason for this, is they are tipped with phosphorous and sulphur (brimstone) elements which release noxious fumes when ignited, and are used in the Black Arts to invoke demonic entities. Striking matches to light candles which have been blessed and charged would therefore seem futile.

Light a small candle in another room, from a butane lighter, or natural gas flame, and carry it to your ritual altar. Then, using the taper or lighting stick, light the other candles with it. If you have Altar candles, these are always lit first. Next light any Astral or Personal candles. Last, visualizing your desires, light the Offertory Purpose candle(s).

Candleburning For Protection

Materials:

- Orange 7-Day Candle
- Protection Oil
- Protection Incense
- Witches' Salt
- Notre Dame Water

Procedure:

1) Anoint the candle with the Protection Oil.
2) Light the candle and burn the Protection Incense.
3) Sprinkle the Witches' Salt in a complete circle around the candle.
4) Place some of the Witches' Salt in a cup containing the Notre Dame Water, add additional water to fill the cup.
5) Sprinkle the mixture around the room particularly to the four compass points and anoint yourself on the forehead and arms with it.
6) After doing all this, chant the following incantation three times:

I call on the Elements,
I call on the Spirit of Protection.
With your help, I am protected;
Put the Light around me.

A Wall of Protection is now about me.
Never shall it be broken.
Please lend your assistance.
The strength of the Light will hold.
So Mote It Be.

Candleburning to Uncross a Person

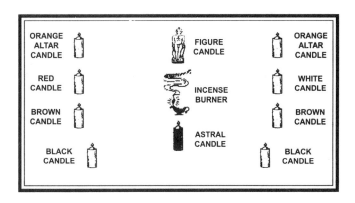

Materials:

- Male or Female Figure Candle *(represents crossed person)*
- Astral Candle - *(represents astral sign of crossed person)*
- Red Candle
- White Candle
- Frank and Myrrh Incense
- Two Orange Altar Candles
- Two Brown candles
- Two Black candles

Procedure:

1) Light the Altar Candles.

2) Light the Frank and Myrrh incense.

3) Light the Astral Candle.

4) Light the Red candle, thinking of strength.

5) Light the White candle, thinking of the crossed condition leaving.

6) Light the Black candles, thinking of the darkness leaving.

7) Light the Brown candles, thinking of the despair leaving.

8) Chant the following, three times:

As the candles burn,
Purity and Strength will be.
The White Light will overcome –
Protection and Strength will be.
So Mote It Be.

11

Candleburning to Protect Against Evil

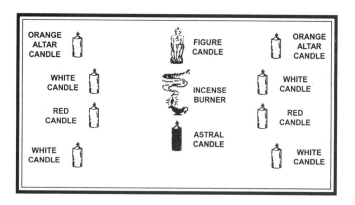

Materials:

- Two Orange Altar Candles
- Two Red candles
- Four White candles
- Astral Candle
- White Figure Candle (represents crossed person)
- Frankincense Incense

Procedure:

1) Light the Altar Candles.
2) Light the Frankincense Incense.
3) Light the Astral Candle. Think of the person surrounded in the bright white light.
4) Light the White candles, thinking of Purity.
5) Light the Red candles, thinking of Strength and Power.
6) Chant the following three times:

White Light of Purity, surround _____ and protect him (or her)
May Truth and the Strength to overcome Be his (hers)
Protect ! Protect! Protect!
May the White Light Surround and protect.
So Mote It Be.

Ritual for Unjinxing a Home or Business

Materials:

- Spool of Red Silk thread
- Four Blue Altar Candles
- Four Thieves' Vinegar
- Witches' Salt
- Chickweed herb
- Mugwort herb

Procedure:

1) Tie the red silk thread around the doorknob the front door of the house or business.
2) Place the Four Thieves' Vinegar in a large pan or jar, add the Witches' Salt, and enough water to fill.
3) Place the Chickweed and Mugwort herbs in the mixture in the bowl and mix well.
4) Place the four Blue candles in the four corners of the house or business building.
5) Light the Blue candles.
6) Sprinkle some of the mixture around the house, and particularly around the candles.
7) Chant the following:

> *A Chain of Power is placed in here.*
> *Revoke all negative forms;*
> *Return all evil.*
> *The thread is a chain;*
> *It shall stop all evil,*
> *With the Power I invoke.*
> *This I say!*
> *So Mote It Be!*

Unhexing Ritual

Materials:

- 1 fresh lemon
- Unhexing Incense
- Unhexing Oil
- Red Conjure bag
- Witches' Salt
- 7-Day Orange candle

Procedure:

1) Anoint the candle and yourself with the Unhexing Oil.
2) Light the candle.
3) Burn some Unhexing Incense.
4) Cut the lemon in half.
5) Sprinkle some of the Witchs' Salt on each half of the lemon.
6) Put the lemon back together and place it in the conjure bag.
7) Put the lemon, still in the bag, outside your front door bury it, if possible.
8) Allow the candle to burn out completely.
9) Anoint yourself with Unhexing Oil each day.

Cleansing and Uncrossing Ritual

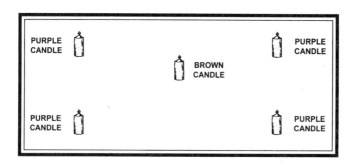

Materials:

- Four Purple candles
- Four Thieves' Vinegar
- One 7-Day Brown candle
- Witches' Salt

Procedure:

1) Light the four Purple candles.
2) Light the Brown candle.
3) Place some of the Four Thieves' Vinegar in a bowl.
4) Add some of the Witches' Salt.
5) Add enough water to fill the bowl.
6) Sprinkle the mixture around the candles.
7) Sprinkle the mixture all around the house.
8) Anoint yourself with it on the forehead and the arms.
9) Chant the following three times:

With this ritual,
I cleanse away all evil;
I cleanse away all negative thoughts.
The power of evil is removed.
As I sprinkle this solution, Evil will go!
Negativity will dissipate.
The powers of evil are removed!
So Mote It Be.

Uncrossing Ritual

Materials:

- Devil's Shoestring
- Mandrake Root
- Guinea Pepper
- King Solomon's Root
- Notre Dame Water
- John The Conqueror Incense
- Jinx Removing Incense
- Van Van Floor Wash
- Uncrossing Bath Wash
- Uncrossing Oil
- Uncrossing Powder
- Jinx Removing Powder
- Witches' Salt
- 7-Day Yellow candle

Procedure:

1) Place some Devil's Shoestring, Mandrake Root, Guinea Pepper and King Solomon's Root in a glass containing the Witches' Salt and some water.

2) Anoint the candle with the Uncrossing Oil, and place some on yourself.

3) Light the 7-Day candle.

4) Burn the Jinx Removing and John the Conqueror Incenses.

5) Sprinkle some of the Uncrossing and Jinx Removing Powders around.

6) Make a wash with the Van Van Floor Wash with water and wash your floors.

7) Take a bath in the Uncrossing Bath Wash.

8) Sprinkle the Notre Dame Water around the house and on yourself.

(Note: repeat all procedures for each day the candle burns).

Jinx Removing Ritual

Materials:

- 7-Day Orange candle
- Jinx Removing Oil
- Jinx Removing Incense
- Jinx Removing Powder

Procedure:

1) Anoint the candle with the Jinx Removing Oil and light it.
2) Burn some of the Jinx Removing Incense.
3) Anoint yourself with Jinx Removing Oil.
4) Sprinkle some of the Jinx Removing Powder around the candle.
5) Chant the following:

> *As the candle burns,*
> *So do all of the jinxes.*
> *None shall remain!*
> *All shall be gone!*
> *So Mote It Be.*

Uncrossing Ritual for Home or Business

Materials:

- Witches' Salt
- John the Conqueror Root
- Cloves
- Mandrake Root
- Basil
- Laurel Leaves
- 7-Day Purple candle
- Uncrossing Incense
- Purple conjure bag

Procedure:

1) Sprinkle some of the Witchs' Salt across your front door.
2) Burn the Uncrossing Incense.
3) Light the candle.
4) Place some of the Witches' Salt, John The Conqueror Root, Clove, Mandrake Root, Basil, Laurel and some of the Uncrossing Incense into the Purple bag.
5) Hang the bag above your front door.
6) Allow the 7-Day Purple candle to burn down completely.
7) Burn up all of the remaining Uncrossing Incense.

Ritual for Removing Evil Spirits

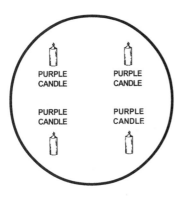

Seal of the Pentagram
(See page 35)

Materials:
- Frank and Myrrh Incense
- Four purple candles
- Seal of the Pentagram (you'll need one for each doorway)
- Holy Oil
- Silver cord

Procedure:
1) Anoint the four Purple candles and yourself with the Holy Oil.
2) Place the four Purple candles in a square.
3) Arrange the Silver cord in a circle, around the candles.
4) Light the candles.
5) Burn the Frank and Myrrh Incense.
6) Chant the following:

> *I exorcise you, Evil Spirits. Flee from this place!*
> *Do not resist, but yield... Depart-Now!*
> *I call on Zeus and Ra,*
> *Help ! O dispel all evil.*
> *With this might, you are beaten.*
> *Begone, all evil!*
> *So Mote It Be.*

7) Place the Seal of the Pentagram over each door.

Ritual to Get Uncrossed

Materials:

- Sea Lettuce or Mullein herb
- Uncrossing Oil
- Uncrossing or Jinx Removing Bath
- Uncrossing Powder
- John The Conqueror Incense
- Confusion Powder

Procedure:

1) Soak some of the Sea Lettuce in salt water in a well-lit place for four days.

2) Sprinkle some of the water around your house, particularly by any doors or windows.

3) Add a little of the water to your bath for seven days.

4) For the next seven days following, add some Uncrossing or Jinx Removing Bath to your tub.

5) Wear a little of the Uncrossing Oil and the Uncrossing Powder on your body for fourteen days.

6) Burn the John The Conqueror Incense during the whole 14 day cycle, for at least one hour each day.

7) Sprinkle Confusion Powder around your house, again concentrating on the doors and windows for the second seven days (you will have sprinkled the Sea Lettuce water around for the first seven).

Miscellaneous Rituals

To Rid Your House of Evil Spirits -
- Hang some Hyssop in a yellow conjure bag above the door.

(Old English-8th century)

To Keep Your Home Free of Evil Spirits -
- Burn a blue beeswax candle at all times.

To Keep a Ghost From Being Mischievous -
- Keep some Bay Leaves or branches in your house on a plate in the center of the dining room.
- Keep a Castor Oil plant live and growing in your home.
- Keep a white Coral Stone on the center table in plain sight.
- Keep a red flower in a black pot in the kitchen.
- Keep some dried Vervain herb in an envelope or conjure bag on your person to ward off negative influences.

(Ancient Greek, Roman and Druidic)

To Absorb a Curse or Negative Sending -
- Use a fresh onion, cut into quarters, and place one quarter in each corner of the room. When the problem has cleared up, take the onion out and bury it, where no one could find it or eat it.

To Return a Curse to the Sender -
- Take a small bottle; half fill it with broken glass, pins and other sharp objects. Then urinate into the bottle, take it outside, and bury it in some secluded place.
- Mix some sulfur with an incense, and burn at midnight-outside your front door to keep evil from entering your house
  (**Note:** *don't breathe the fumes yourself, they're very irritating*).

Herbs, Oils, Incense, Powders, Floorwashes and Salts

Herbs

The magic powers of herbs are brought to life by the state of your mind. You can use herbs in making amulets or charms, and in many rituals which are designed to assist you in your work. Herbs are useful in reaching your goals in sex, love, money, revenge or success. The power of concentration is the most important factor of the mind, and the positive thinking of an individual accomplishing the magic is truly a feat of the mind's magic.

You have the ability to control your thoughts to enable fulfillment in your life, and to make that life a simple affair. Herbs assist you in becoming a *"point of concentration"* which enables you to *"send"* your thoughts.

As you make any herbal charm, you must think in a positive way, *"seeing"* the desired result as something already done. Keep a steady faith, and avoid all doubt and fear; then your wish will be fulfilled.

Historically, herbal potions are old; they are even recorded from the time of the pyramids, and there are many references by ancient Greeks, Celts, Druids, Arabs, as well as the Egyptians. Herbs have the magical power in them, but with the power of your positive thinking, the power grows stronger.

Herbal charms are usually kept in a conjure bag, or, in the case of a root or nut, on a chain. In some circumstances they may be carried loose in a pocket or purse.

Following is a list of some of the more common herbs used for uncrossing, jinx removing or banishing negative influences; along with some suggestions for their effective use.

Ague Weed - Mix with Frankincense and burn to break the power of a hex.

Angelica - Sprinkle around your home to protect against evil spirits, or wear as a charm on your person for the same purpose.

Bay Leaves - Place several leaves around your home as a protection against black witchcraft.

Betony - Sprinkle around your home to protect against evil spirits. May also be worn on the person as a charm against evil.

Bladderwrack- Carry some on your person for protection.

Blood Root- Place around your home, especially by window sills or doorways for protection against evil.

Boldo Leaves- Use as above.

Cinquefoil - Place some in a white conjure bag and keep in a dark place in your home, to ward off evil spirits.

Clover - Soak in salt water for four days, then sprinkle the water around your home to ward off evil spirits.

Comfrey Root - Keep some with you for protection while traveling.

Dill - Mix with some salt water and scatter around your house, to break negative magic.

Clover - Soak in salt water for four days, then sprinkle the water around your home to ward off evil spirits.

Comfrey Root - Keep some with you for protection while traveling.

Dill - Mix with some salt water and scatter around your house, to break negative magic.

Elm Bark - Put some in a box and keep in a dark place to stop malicious gossip.

5-Finger Grass - Put some in a white conjure bag and hang over your bed, to ensure pleasant dreams.

Balm of Gilead Buds - Carry some in a white conjure bag on your person, to protect against curses and hexes.

Holy Herb - Add some to your bath water to protect against evil.

Lucky Hand Root - Wear on your person for protection.

Marjoram - Place some in each room of your house; evil cannot bear the odor.

Mint - Keep a jar of mint (with the lid off) in a dark room in your home; evil spirits will leave.

Mistletoe - Keep a sprig on your person; keeps evil witches away.

Monkshood - Keep on your person; protects against devils and demons (***Note:*** *keep out of the reach of children and pets. It is poisonous).*

Mullein - Sew some into your pillow; keeps nightmares away.

Poke Root- Brew into a tea; washes evil out of your body.

Pearl Moss - Sprinkle some at your front door; only Good will enter.

Queen of the Meadow - Keep in a dark place; keeps evil ghosts away.

Trumpet Weed - Put some in a white conjure bag and wear on your person to protect yourself from evil (***Note:*** *also a poison be careful!)*

Wahoo Root - Boil some in some salt water, then add to your bath. Drives evil spirits away.

Oils

Oils have been used for many centuries for magical purposes, and it should be pointed out that a difference does exist between oils, perfumes and essences. Oils are mixtures of the extracts of herbs in their purest form. Perfumes and essences are dilutions of the oils, and therefore, will be weaker in their power. I strongly recommend that only the oil form be used by anyone who is serious in his or her practice.

Any of the following oils may be used for uncrossing or jinx removing at any time - either by themselves, in combination, or with any of the appropriate rituals. You may wear the oil as a body oil or perfume, or use as indicated in the instructions for the various rituals. Oils add power to any magic work, and should be seriously considered.

Uncrossing Oil - A powerful blend to uncross or unhex and protect. To rid your home of crossed conditions, add nine drops to water. Sprinkle it throughout your home for nine consecutive days. Sprinkle some outside your home at the doorway on the last day.

Uncrossing/Jinx Removing - A double action oil. Remove both crossed and jinxed conditions. Dress a White Candle and anoint your palms and you will see your luck turn around.

Unhexing Oil - To get rid of a hex or evil spirit, anoint your temples and your body. Add it to your bath and anoint the frames of your doors and windows.

Jinx Killer - Change your bad luck to good luck. Wear this oil and sprinkle it in your home, transportation and at work.

Jinx Removing - For everyone in a crossed condition. Anoint your temple and forehead each day. Draw a religious symbol such as a cross on the path to your door for added strength.

Jinx Removing/Fast Luck - A double action oil. Remove jinxes and turns your luck around to good. Dress a White Candle with this oil or wear it on your body.

Holy - A sacred oil. To bring success and blessings, utilize the oil on altars, talisman, candles, incense and yourself. Use it with faith and prayer to help those who are ill. Rub it on candles to purify your space.

Home Protection - Sprinkle around your home to protect from evil spirits. Anoint any charm or talisman used for the same purpose. Anoint the seal from the 6th and 7th Books of Moses called the Great Pentagram and carry it with you.

Seven African Powers - A powerful oil which calls on the assistance of the Seven African Deities for help with a variety of matters including love, money, luck and peace of mind. When a situation is desperate take a bath with the oil added, anoint your body and say a prayer to the Seven African Spirits once a day for three consecutive days.

Seven Day Uncrossing - To free yourself of a burden. Each morning for 7 days, anoint your wrists, ankles and heart with this oil. Focus your intent on positive thoughts of what you want.

Angel - When you use this oil it attracts all forms of spirits from the other realms. Use it to call in the aid of spirits. Angels are attracted to the scent, so place it on your altar or in your "work" room.

Angelica - Magickally good for all forms of protection, exorcism and to remove curses and hexes. Sprinkle in the four corners of your house to get rid of evil, or, when added to incense it speeds up your natural healing process.

Allspice - Spiritual vibrations are associated with the oil. Use to anoint altars and in rituals. Adds power. When you are focused on your intent, it will help you to succeed. Placed on your forehead, it will aid in divination. Placed on the soles of your feet and naval, it will give you strength, will-power, and drive.

Ju Ju - Comes down through time to us from Africa. Very powerful for hex breaking or making. If worn daily, no hex can be put on you. When sprinkled or put on a person, it will make them go away if you focus on seeing the person leave in a positive way.

Babel - To cause confusion and hex, throw on the doorstep of an enemy (but remember what you do, positive or negative work comes back to you).

Devil - A crossing oil. Used for hexing and jinxing when put in an enemy's path.

Devil's Master - It will give you control over the negative intentions of other people. Anoint a White Candle and a Seal of Fire, then carry the Seal and a small piece of the left over candle with you at all times, after burning it.

Devil's Shoestring - When used for protection and luck, anoint a devil's shoestring and carry it with you.

Fiery Wall of Protection - Breaks hexes and jinxes. Very powerful protection oil. Protects from accidents and problems when worn daily.

Five Finger Grass - Protects you from harm. Anoint yourself and wherever you are; boat, train, home, car, etc.

Flaming Power - Protection from evil. Wear it to overcome those who wish you harm. When you travel, anoint yourself and your luggage, you will be assured a safe trip.

Nutmeg - A great breaker of evil hexes. Brings the best of luck to all users. Anoint one Blue candle and one White candle and say a prayer for protection. Brings luck to you when you anoint a charm.

Rose Geranium - Breaks hexes and protects against them. Should you need protection, anoint your body and your home, car or workplace. Use it on altars for Blessings.

Wormwood - Although known as a hexing oil, more of its' uses are positive. To break a hex, pour some of the oil into flowing water, such as a stream or a water faucet.

Rue - Breaks hexes and jinxes. Anoint a White Conjure bag with it so nobody can put a curse on you. Carry the bag with you at all times. Exorcism rituals have more power with Rue Oil added. Add to bath water to calm emotional distress.

Run Devil Run - It is said that the devil cannot stand this smell, so it will keep him away. Anoint your doorway and window frames and windows to keep the devil out of your life. Say protection prayer.

Incenses

Incenses are important ingredients for any ritual or even by themselves. They may be burned at any time in the home, either alone or in combination, and they will definitely enhance any ceremony. Even used alone, they will exert a positive influence to help you, when there is no time or convenience for a proper ritual.

1 - Jinx Removing	**7** - Domination
2 - Uncrossing	**8** - Confusion
3 - Unhexing	**9** - Lilac
4 - Bible	**10** - Satan Be Gone
5 - Holy	**11** - Temple
6 - Angel	**12** - Frankincense

Note: While the above may be used in any combination, some mixtures are better than others. Numbers 4, 5, 6, 9 and 12 are to attract Higher, Positive Powers for your protection. A combination or mixture using them is better not mixed with numbers 1, 2, 3, 7, 8 or 10 - all of which are to hamper, restrict or banish Negative Forces working against you. Number 11, Temple Incense, is to sanctify the premises, and may be used with either group.

Powders

Powders are very potent, and can be sprinkled around the entrances, windows and inside to help in the ritual work. They may be used on the body and in other ways, as indicated in the various ritual instructions.

• Jinx Removing	• Domination
• Uncrossing	• Confusion
• Unhexing	• Lilac
• Bible	• Satan Be Gone
• Holy	• Temple
• Angel	

Refer to the note above when using powders in combination.

Washes and Salts

Floor Washes

Washing your floor with one of the following washes will bring a fresh start with no negative influences.

- Uncrossing
- Unhexing
- Jinx Removing

Bath Washes

By bathing in the following baths, you will wash away evil.

- Jinx Removing
- Uncrossing
- Unhexing

Hand Wash Soaps

- Jinx Removing
- Uncrossing
- Unhexing

Bath Salts

Bath Salts are good as concentrates, and easy to use - just add a handful to your bath.

- Jinx Removing
- Uncrossing
- Unhexing

Seals

A Seal is a design which is, in effect, a magical incantation or invocation, inscribed on a sheet of paper, for a specific reason or purpose.

The Seal is a potent magical tool, copy it yourself by hand (Xerox or printed copies won't work), to bring to you the forces and effects the Seal represents.

In making Seals, as in all "magic" workings, your own mind is the most important power of all. Your intent must be clear and undivided - you can't be thinking of your hairdo, your grocery list, or anything except what you're doing and why you're doing it - and you must have confidence . . . FAITH! . . . in your Work. Visualize the desired result clearly in your "mind's eye". This sort of "positive thinking", coupled with the work, will insure the fulfillment of your wish.

You will find, on the pages following, traditional Seals for uncrossing or jinx removing. If you desire to design your own, good texts with the basic information may be purchased at any good Occult bookstore - such as the one where you obtained this booklet.

Magic Square of the Sun Talisman

Used by Witches and Ceremonial Magicians to attract the enlightening and protective powers of that planet to a ritual.

6	32	3	34	35	1
7	11	27	28	8	30
19	14	16	15	23	24
18	20	22	21	17	13
25	29	10	9	26	12
36	5	33	4	2	31

Procedure:

1) Draw a square on a piece of parchment paper.

2) Divide the Square into thirty-six boxes, as above.

3) Fill in the numbers, in their natural order-that is, find the number one in the sample, then put it in the same place in your Square; look for number two, and do the same. Then fill in three, and so on. As you fill in each number, chant:

> "Thou Sun, Giver of Light, Banisher of Evil,
> Guard and Protect me always. "

4) With the last number - 36 - add:

> "So Mote It Be. "

5) Before doing any Ritual or Spell for Protection or Uncrossing, take out the Square (which you should keep, wrapped in gold or yellow cloth, in a safe place) and look at each number in turn-still in their natural order. Then proceed with the Working.

Seal of Solomon
Fourth Pentacle of the Moon

This image drawn on parchment paper with Dove's Blood ink defends its owner from all evil and from any injury to body or soul. Carry it with you, use it in rituals, or hang over your door. Anoint it with any protective oil.

Fourth Pentacle of the Moon

Seal of Solomon
Sixth Pentacle of Mars

The owner of this talisman cannot be harmed. The enemy who attempts to inflict harm, either physically or spiritually, shall have their weapons turned against them. Draw the image on parchment paper with Dove's Blood ink, carry it with you at all times. Anoint it with Protection Oil.

Sixth Pentacle of Mars

Jinx Removing Seal

Procedure:

1) Copy this Seal onto a piece of parchment paper, using Dove's Blood Ink.
2) Anoint the Seal and yourself with Jinx Removing Oil.
3) Place the completed Seal under a Yellow candle, and burn the candle.
4) Put the Seal in a Red conjure bag, and carry it with you. Do not let anyone else touch the bag.

Seal of Uncrossing

Procedure:

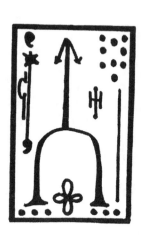

1) Copy this Seal onto a piece of parchment paper, using Dove's Blood Ink.
2) Anoint the Seal and yourself with Uncrossing Oil.
3) Put the Seal into a Purple conjure bag.
4) Hang the bag over your front door.

Seal of Protection

(Relates to protection from the influences of others - whether people or spirits).

Procedure:

1) Copy this Seal with Dove's Blood Ink onto a piece of parchment paper.

2) Put the Seal in a small Red conjure bag.

3) Anoint the bag with Protection Oil.

4) Carry the bag with you at all times. (Note: This seal is the Pentagram referred to in the Ritual on page 19 of this booklet. You may want to make several, in case you need that particular ritual some time).

Table of Astral Colors

Sign	For Those Born Between. . .	Astral Colors
Aquarius	January 20—February 18	Blue
Pisces	February 19—March 20	White
Aries	March 21—April 19	Pink
Taurus	April 20—May 20	Yellow
Gemini	May 21—June 21	Red
Cancer	June 22—July 22	Green
Leo	July 23—August 22	Red
Virgo	August 23—September 22	Gold
Libra	September 23—October 22	Black
Scorpio	October 23—November 21	Brown
Sagittarius	November 22—December 21	Yellow
Capricorn	December 22—January 19	Red

Miscellany of Uncrossing

Colors	Yellow, Orange, Brown
Gems	Lapis, Crystal, Ruby, Garnet, Carnelian, any Yellow gemstone-Amber, etc.
Flowers	Lavender, Dogwood, White Rose
Day	Sunday
Months	March, August
Astrological Sign	Leo
Planet	Sun
Food	Roots (Potato, Yam, Carrot, etc.)
Number	3
Incense	Frankincense, any Uncrossing, Unhexing, Unjinxing

Colors of Jinx Removing

Colors are very important, and should be taken very seriously. You should pick the one which has the best vibrations to assist you in your ritual and develop the most power. A combination of colors might be considered to help you, and the right combination is essential.

The colors of protection are:

- Yellow
- Orange
- Brown

Yellow and orange are positive vibrations; they help to attract positive forces of protection and energy to you. Brown is a negative vibration, and is useful to banish or get rid of the negative forces which are causing your problems.

These colors give you the right balance to protect yourself, and to return any jinx or crossed condition placed against you.

Numbers

Numbers have a history of deep and recognized magical powers. The right number, at the right time, will concentrate the cosmic vibrations which will help you most.

When the number 3 is associated with a conjure bag, a seal or a talisman, it strengthens the object with the Light, the Lifegiving and the Evil Banishing powers of the Sun.

You might consider incorporating the mystical "three" into your work; draw it on the back of your seals, or draw it on a piece of good parchment paper to add to your conjure bag. Dove's Blood Ink is preferable.

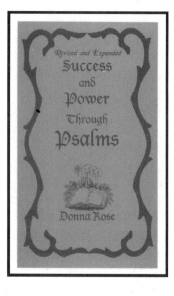

ITEM #224
$6.95

Revised and Expanded

Success and Power
Through Psalms

By Donna Rose

For thousands of years, men and women have found in the Psalms the
perfect prayer book, possessing wisdom applicable to every human
situation. Wise men and women of deep mystical insight have also
learned to decipher the magical formulas David and the other Psalmists
hid behind the written words. These formulas help the seeker solve
everyday problems, achieve higher states of consciousness, gain
material and spiritual wealth, as well as help defend himself or herself
against psychic attacks and all manner of dangers.

The Revised and Expanded edition of Donna Rose's classic offers over
300 simple to perform magical rituals to help you manifest all of your
desires using the magical powers of the psalms.

ISBN 0-942272-79-X 5½"x 8½ $6.95

SPIRITUAL CLEANSINGS & PSYCHIC DEFENSES

By Robert Laremy

Psychic attacks are real and their effects can be devastating to the victim. Negative vibrations can be as harmful as bacteria, germs and viruses. There are time-honored methods of fighting these insidious and pernicious agents of distress. These techniques are described in this book and they can be applied by you. No special training or supernatural powers are needed to successfully employ these remedies. All of the procedures described in this book are safe and effective, follow the instructions without the slightest deviation. The cleansings provided are intended as *"over-the-counter"* prescriptions to be used by anyone being victimized by these agents of chaos.

ISBN 0-942272-72-2 5½"x 8½" 112 pages $9.95